50 One-Minute Tips for Recruiting Employees

Finding the Right People for Your Organization

David K. Hayes, Ph.D. and
Jack D. Ninemeier, Ph.D.

A Fifty-Minute™ Series Book

1-800-442-7477

CrispLearning.com

50 One-Minute Tips for Recruiting Employees

Finding the Right People for Your Organization

David K. Hayes, Ph.D. and Jack D. Ninemeier, Ph.D.

CREDITS:
Senior Editor: **Debbie Woodbury**
Editor: **Luann Rouff**
Production Manager: **Judy Petry**
Design: **Nicole Phillips**
Production Artist: **Zach Hooker**
Cartoonist: **James McFarlane**

Printed in the United States of America by Von Hoffmann Graphics, Inc.

CrispLearning.com

01 02 03 04 10 9 8 7 6 5 4 3 2 1

Library of Congress Catalog Card Number 2001092372
Hayes, David K. and Jack D. Ninemeier
50 One-Minute Tips for Recruiting Employees
ISBN 1-56052-645-9

Learning Objectives For:

50 ONE-MINUTE TIPS FOR RECRUITING EMPLOYEES

The objectives for *50 One-Minute Tips for Recruiting Employees* are listed below. They have been developed to guide you, the reader, to the core issues covered in this book.

THE OBJECTIVES OF THIS BOOK ARE:

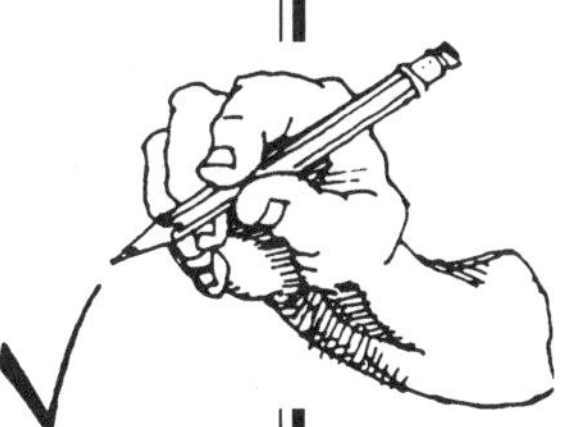

- ❑ 1) To outline procedures for planning and implementing effective recruitment strategies
- ❑ 2) To describe simple and effective recruitment techniques
- ❑ 3) To present special tactics for recruiting young persons
- ❑ 4) To offer strategies for recruiting older workers, those in career transition, legal immigrants, and other classes of potentially eligible applicants
- ❑ 5) To describe basic techniques for screening job applicants
- ❑ 6) To define methods for selecting new employees

ASSESSING YOUR PROGRESS

In addition to the learning objectives, Crisp Learning has developed an **assessment** that covers the fundamental information presented in this book. A 25-item, multiple-choice and true-false questionnaire allows the reader to evaluate his or her comprehension of the subject matter. To learn how to obtain a copy of this assessment, please call **1-800-442-7477** and ask to speak with a Customer Service Representative.

Assessments should not be used in any employee selection process.

About the Authors

David K. Hayes is the managing owner of a hotel in Lansing Michigan. He has over 25 years experience in directing employees at all levels of experience in the hospitality business. David is also the Editor of HospitalityLawyer.com, a website devoted to the legal, safety, and security information needs of the hospitality industry.

He received his Bachelor of Science (B.S.), Masters (M.S.) in Restaurant, Hotel, and Institutional Management, and a Ph.D. in Education from Purdue University. He is an accomplished author and trainer who has published popular university textbooks in the areas of hospitality business law, cost control, and employee training.

Jack D. Ninemeier is a professor at Michigan State University's The School of Hospitality Business. He is the author, co-author, or editor of 28 books relating to the food-service and healthcare industries. He has also authored more than 175 trade journal articles.

He received his Ph.D. from the University of Wisconsin. He is a Certified Hotel Administrator (C.H.A.), Certified Food and Beverage Executive (C.F.B.E.), and Certified Hospitality Educator (C.H.E.) as recognized by the American Hotel and Lodging Association.

Dedication

This book is dedicated to managers in all types of organizations who are confronted with the challenges of recruiting, selecting, and retaining the staff needed to properly serve their customers. It is also dedicated to Brother Herman Zaccarelli, C.S.C., whose guidance and faith in the humanity of managers everywhere, and whose beliefs about the dignity of work and life-long education, have made him an exceptional friend and colleague.

Preface

One of the most critical skills for operating a successful organization is the ability to recruit, select, and retain a skilled and motivated workforce. As business owners compete for entry-level and professional employees, they must be very creative in developing strategies to attract new staff members to their organizations.

Surprisingly little has been written about ways to address this issue, although it confronts the majority of those who manage either for-profit or not-for-profit organizations. Often, the managers responsible for filling entry-level positions may, themselves, have only recently been hired for or promoted to their job. Therefore, mid-level managers and higher-level executives must provide their subordinate managers with the tools needed to meet these recruitment and retention challenges. To be effective in today's increasingly competitive labor market, managers must be equipped and trained to:

- ➤ Recruit the most qualified applicants
- ➤ Establish policies and procedures that allow the best applicants to be selected

This book is full of ideas that will help you perform these essential tasks. Some tips will be more applicable than others for your particular situation and staffing needs. Many can be adapted, with a little creativity, to suit a wide range of business scenarios. We encourage you to experiment with the tips; perhaps they will inspire you to develop some unique recruiting strategies of your own. If so, please share them with us (see page 109).

Good luck and happy hiring!

David K. Hayes

Jack D. Ninemeier

Contents

Strategy 3: Develop "Youth Appeal"

Strategy 4: Foster Workplace Diversity

Strategy 5: Screen to Ensure Success

Strategy 6: Start Smart–Employee Selection and Orientation

STRATEGY 1

Do Your Homework

Tip 1: Build Respect and Become an "Employer of Choice"

People will want to work for you if you have a reputation as a good employer. Why might someone want to work for you? Why would someone be less likely to seek a job with your organization than another? An analysis of the way you treat your present employees will help address these questions.

Perhaps the single most important "ingredient" in your recruitment strategy is the extent to which you show *genuine* respect for your current employees. You demonstrate your respect for your employees when you:

- Provide them with the necessary initial training and ongoing coaching that enables them to be successful
- Allow them to provide significant input to work-related decisions that affect them
- Empower them to make decisions that affect your customers
- Give them the opportunity to experience pride and joy in their jobs

Most successful organizations have established an image in the public's mind. Customers of national chains know what to expect when they rent a video, eat a meal, purchase clothing, or have their carpet cleaned. You can use the same approach whether you are a small business owner or affiliated with a multi-unit organization.

Begin your examination of *recruitment* strategies by analyzing your *retention* strategies.* It is easy for applicants to spot a prospective employer who is "trying to fill a position," rather than recruiting a new member for his or her team. Employee respect should be interwoven throughout all recruitment strategies.

When a prominent feature of your organization is "We respect our employees, and we are the employer of choice in our community," a giant step in the recruitment process has already been taken. Many organizations have reputations as good, average, or poor places to work. How do you think your organization is currently regarded by prospective applicants?

---

* *Read* 50 One-Minute Tips for Retaining Employees, *by David K. Hayes and Jack D. Ninemeier, Crisp Publications, 2001.*

RATE YOUR RESPECT IQ

Respect refers to honor and to an expression of consideration and courtesy. Successful employers genuinely respect their staff. This encourages employees to stay longer and contribute more. Think about your staff when answering the following questions.

1. Rate the level of respect that you generally show for your employees.

   ❑ High ❑ ❑ Average ❑ ❑ Low

2. Rate the level of respect that your employees generally show for you.

   ❑ High ❑ ❑ Average ❑ ❑ Low

3. Is there a correlation between the levels of respect you identified in Questions 1 and 2?

   ❑ Yes ❑ No

   (You'll often find that your employees respect you to about the same extent that you respect them!)

4. List three things you currently do to show your genuine respect for your staff members.

   ____

   ____

   ____

5. Describe three additional things you can do to show your employees that you genuinely respect them.

   ____

   ____

   ____

Tip 2: Understand Loyalty and Commitment

Loyalty and commitment are perceived differently in today's workplace than in the past. Today's employee/employer relationship is similar to a business partnership. Both partners will stay in the relationship only as long as it is in their own best interests to do so.

You can't provide lifetime employment, and your workers know it. Many younger workers have grown up in households with economic uncertainty. These youth are frequently fiercely independent and realistic. Older workers have been reorganized, reengineered and downsized to the point that their trust is also in themselves, rather than in their places of employment.

Today's workers can and will exhibit loyalty if you provide them with a reason to do so. Offer your employees portable skills and realistic opportunities to continue to develop their own careers, both now and in the future. Be certain that the entry-level workers you are recruiting know how the jobs they are doing today will benefit them in the future.

What Do You Offer?

Assume you have worked at one of your company's entry-level positions for one year.

Describe three skills you will have learned or the knowledge areas that should have increased during that time:

1. ____
2. ____
3. ____

Are these skills and knowledge areas you could likely use at your next job?

❑ Yes ❑ No

If not, describe something you could do to enhance this position's opportunities for growth.

____

____

Tip 3: Keep Your Strategies Current

Effective recruiters know that they cannot always use the same tactics to recruit applicants from different groups of potential employees. When recruiting different types of staff members, it is important to know which tactics work and which don't. Now is the time to fine-tune your current recruitment strategies. Continue to use those that have been effective; and eliminate those that aren't. Once you understand what works, you can build on that foundation with the ideas in this book. Use your proven tactics while you test others.

Update your current recruitment strategies

Do some tactics that worked previously seem less effective today?

❑ Yes ❑ No

If yes, how can you update these tactics to be more effective?

____

____

Do you tend to use the same tactics over and over?

❑ Yes ❑ No

If yes, what else might be effective for your organization?

____

____

When is the last time you tried a new and creative tactic? What was it? Was it effective? Why or why not?

____

____

Tip 4: Identify the Requirements of Each Position

Every job has basic requirements. These critical components are among the most important factors applicants evaluate when considering work offers. Your goal is to encourage the widest possible candidate pool when establishing these basic elements. The more flexible you can be when establishing minimum job requirements, the greater the number of applicants eligible for your positions.

Ask yourself how much flexibility you can truly offer in the following areas:

- ➤ Shift start and end times
- ➤ Experience required
- ➤ Education required
- ➤ Hours worked daily
- ➤ Hours worked weekly
- ➤ Weekend work requirements
- ➤ Variety of tasks
- ➤ Walking, standing, lifting, or other physical requirements
- ➤ Need to work alone or with others
- ➤ Dress or uniform requirements
- ➤ Other: ____

Identify the requirements of your jobs, and document what can and cannot be changed. Consider, for example, an entry-level clerical position that has always begun at 8:00 A.M. Assume that there is a single mother in your community who:

- ➤ Needs a job
- ➤ Is highly qualified for this open position
- ➤ Has midmorning and afternoon daycare available
- ➤ Is responsible for taking her children to school at 8:15 A.M.

Would you consider revising the starting and ending times for this position to accommodate the qualified applicant?

❑ Yes ❑ No ❑ Maybe

Careful consideration of each position's basic requirements will enable you to determine "necessary" rather than "nice-to-have" requirements. This will help you to find and retain the best candidates eligible for your open positions.

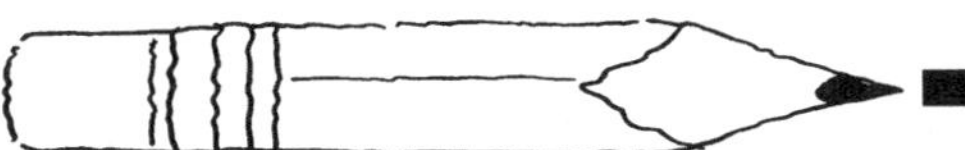

Rate Your Flexibility

Evaluate an entry-level position for which you have recently recruited applicants. First, consider the requirements you have historically considered critical; then creatively think of ways you can be more flexible.

Position: ____

Job Characteristics	Current	Future
Start time		
Stop time		
Experience required		
Education required		
Hours worked per day		
Hours worked per week		
Weekend work requirements		
Variety of tasks within the job		
Walking, standing, lifting, or other physical requirements		
Need to work alone or with others		
Dress or uniform requirements		
Other:		

Tip 5: Identify the Best Features of Your Jobs

Clearly identify and communicate the best features of the jobs you offer. Applicants often misunderstand and/or stereotype some jobs. "Jobs in fast-food restaurants are hot and greasy" and "Jobs in grocery stores are boring" reflect perceptions that may not be accurate. You must compete against other businesses for the best workers. You can compete most effectively by identifying the desirable aspects of your jobs.

To identify the best features of your place of employment, talk to your current workers. What do they like best? What makes them want to stay? Create a one-page handout entitled "Top Ten Reasons to be a (insert job title) at (insert the name of your organization)!" Include this document in your "recruitment package" provided to every applicant (see Tip 8). If you offer several types of jobs, develop a separate list for each. Continue to update your lists, revising them as you improve the quality of your jobs! These lists identify the reasons why your jobs are great; they are among your best promotional tools.

Strut Your Stuff! (Part 1)

In the following space, list five features that you can use to encourage candidates to apply for a position in your organization.

Job Title: ______________________________

1. ______________________________
2. ______________________________
3. ______________________________
4. ______________________________
5. ______________________________

Ask several employees to evaluate the features you have identified, and to contribute additional ideas. Be honest and thorough; factors that appeal to some employees may not appeal to others. When recruiting from a diverse pool of potential applicants, the longest possible list may be the most helpful.

Tip 6: Identify the Best Features of Your Organization

Job seekers have a choice as to where they will work. High school students can be clerks in a video or clothing store. They can be restaurant servers or cooks, or they can work in an athletic club or a convenience store. Even if they know the position they want, they have alternatives. If they want to be a sales clerk, they can apply at several different businesses.

Imagine that you own or are the manager of one of these stores. Imagine also that the type and amount of work an employee does is similar to that of your competitors. Lastly, imagine that all stores in your area pay approximately the same amount for this job. Now ask yourself the following question:

Why would an employee want to work for me, rather than someone else?

The answer to this question can be your single most important recruiting tool, especially when the labor market is tight. All employers say that their organization is a good place to work. Similar pay for similar jobs is an economic reality that most managers face. To be truly competitive, you must know and be able to communicate why your organization is the employer of choice.

Strut Your Stuff! (Part 2)

Why do you work for your organization? Why did your current employees choose it? List five reasons *why* your organization is the best choice for a potential employee.

1. ____________________
2. ____________________
3. ____________________
4. ____________________
5. ____________________

Ask your employees to help develop your list of best features. Create another handout for the recruitment package you will develop in Tip 8.

Tip 7: Ensure that Job Titles Reflect the Jobs

Develop job titles that are meaningful to your employees. Consider Latoya, who manages employees in a video store. Each staff member does similar work. The job titles, however, reflect the length of service and responsibility levels of each employee:

Length of Service	Job Title
1–30 days	Assistant Service Agent
31–180 days	Service Agent
181–365 days	Senior Service Agent
366+ days	Service Agent Supervisor

These title changes reflect the ways in which entry-level employees can progress within Latoya's organization. Compensation and/or benefits should be tied to these job title changes.

Job title changes can be based on any worker achievement, including length of service, exemplary performance, and/or the acquisition of required knowledge and skills. Job titles are not mere words, they are powerful tools; ensure that they make sense, and you will have a strategy in place that benefits your organization and your employees.

Rate Your Job Titles

Consider one of your own positions. What job titles do you use to demonstrate progression in that job?

If you don't currently have any progressive titles in place, now is the time to implement some.

Current Job Title	Achievement/ Length of Service	New Title
________________	________________	________________
________________	________________	________________
________________	________________	________________

Tip 8: Develop a Recruitment Package

Consider the following three scenarios:

- ➤ You are invited to attend a recruitment fair or to speak to a high school, a junior college, or a university class about employment opportunities in your industry.
- ➤ Someone walks into your place of business and asks if you have a position opening.
- ➤ You ask current employees to discuss with their friends employment opportunities with your organization.

What type of information can you make available in these and related situations, and what is the best way to present and deliver your information? A *recruitment package* helps you organize and assemble the information necessary to inform potential applicants about your organization and the positions for which you are recruiting. It can help make your recruitment efforts consistently informative; everyone will learn the same thing, and everything they learn will be what you believe to be most important.

The recruitment package can range from a single sheet of information to a large binder that includes a brochure, a fact sheet, and other work-related materials. If you don't have one, begin simply. Over time, revise your recruitment package as you discover the type of information most critical and helpful to applicants. (You will review your recruitment package again in Tip 48.) Be sure to ask your current employees what information they think would be of interest to potential employees.

Design a Recruitment Package

Use the following checklist to identify components for your recruitment package and complete the table for those components you will use.

Package Element	Include?		If Yes, Necessary Actions		
	Yes	No	Already Available	Need to Develop Who	By When
Company brochure or fact sheet that provides a general description of your organization					
Recruitment brochure that includes: • current job descriptions • essential requirements of jobs (see Tip 4) • best features of jobs (see Tip 5) • best features of your company (see Tip 6) • employee compensation worksheet (see Tip 9)					
Copies of recent job advertisements					
Copies of endorsements from several current employees					
Job application form					
Business cards with information about the best time to call your business					
Map of your business location(s)					
Bus route map with location of your business(es)					
Brief list of employee benefits (i.e., meals, insurance discounts, etc.)					
INS I-9 form (with application)					
1–5 year career path					

Tip 9: Make Your Total Compensation Competitive

Employees want fair pay, and they deserve it. They also want reasonable benefits in keeping with the jobs they hold and with the organization for which they work. Pay plus benefits equals total compensation, and employees can compare the total compensation you pay with that of your competitors.

If you don't control the hourly rates paid, you must ensure that your boss knows the hourly pay rates offered by your competitors.

Some organizations may try to lure your workers away with higher hourly rates of pay. They may, however, offer fewer benefits. Make sure your applicants and current employees know the value of *all* the monetary compensation received as a result of working in your organization. Provide this information to applicants during their initial job interview, to new employees during orientation programs, and to current employees in regular update meetings. If you have made a commitment to provide benefits, identify them and post them in a highly visible place, such as a lunch room or company bulletin board.

Review your organization's total compensation. For a helpful worksheet to calculate the total benefits you currently offer, see the companion book to this one, *50 One-Minute Tips for Retaining Employees,* Crisp Publications.

Tip 10: Use a "Cafeteria Plan" for Bonus Benefits

Do you or can you offer a "cafeteria plan" that provides employees with a choice of benefits that you obtain at low cost? For example, perhaps an amount equal to two or three hours of pay can be allocated monthly to a cafeteria plan for each staff member. Employees could choose the "bonus" benefit(s) they desire. For example, assume you could barter movie tickets valued at $9 for $5. Assume also that you could negotiate discounts for pizza parties, video rentals, spa services, sporting events or other recreational activities, and/or other products or services desired by your employees. At month's end, employees who are "qualified" (for example, have been employed for at least a minimum time and/or who have worked all scheduled shifts) could select from this cafeteria plan of bonus benefits.

While compensation above a specified amount is not necessarily motivation for accepting a job or remaining at a job, a choice of fun bonus benefits is another tool to help you position your company as an employer of choice.

Create Your Bonus Benefit Plan

Consider the amount which you can allocate for a cafeteria bonus benefit program (for example, [average hourly rate] times [2 or 3] = _____).

Step 1. Describe some alternative benefits that your employees would like that fit within this budget. (Ask your employees for suggestions.)

____

____

____

Step 2. What must an employee do to be eligible for a "cafeteria" bonus during the designated time period?

- ❏ Work overtime as needed
- ❏ Achieve specific length of service milestone
- ❏ No unexcused absences
- ❏ Attain specific performance standard(s)
- ❏ Receive customer "kudos"
- ❏ Achieve acceptable performance evaluation
- ❏ Arrive at work on time
- ❏ Arrive at work in proper uniform
- ❏ Complete requested training program
- ❏ Other

Tip 11: Remember That You're Not Alone–Seek Allies

Whether they know it or not, managers in employer-of-choice organizations already have a team of experts available to help plan and deliver recruitment tactics: *current staff members.* This team has a personal stake in finding new team members; your team may have already helped with activities suggested earlier in this book.

In addition to internal allies, you likely have external allies to help solve your recruitment puzzle:

Join your local Chamber of Commerce

Chamber membership can be a critical part of your efforts to make your company known in the community as an employer-of-choice.

Chamber members benefit from business enhancement programs, networking opportunities, timely publications, and seminars addressing local economic data and best management practices. Join the Chamber with the intention of taking advantage of all the programs offered that relate to your business. If you are a supervisor whose own manager is a Chamber member, ask about attending some sessions.

Learn About Your Local Chamber of Commerce

1. Find the telephone number of your local Chamber: ________________
2. Get information about the following:
   - ❑ Chamber goals, purposes, and programs:
   - ❑ Membership:
   - ❑ Meeting times/locations:
   - ❑ Available information regarding generic recruitment strategies:
   - ❑ Other assistance they suggest
   - ❑ Names and telephone numbers of others whom the Chamber representative(s) suggest you contact:

Name	Telephone Number
________________	________________
________________	________________
________________	________________

Join applicable trade associations

Whether you manage a restaurant, a hotel, a hardware store, a nursing home, or an amusement park, almost every segment of government and business has associations of members from similar organizations. In addition, numerous "generic" organizations address disciplines such as management, sales, and so on. Because the primary purpose of professional associations is to help their membership, recruitment concerns will likely be addressed in periodicals, conferences, training sessions, and other venues. While there are no "secrets" to successful recruitment, persons active in your own industry are just like you; they know the "hits, runs, and misses" of recruitment and are willing to share their experiences with others.

Learn About Your Professional Association(s)

1. What national or local professional association(s) represent your industry? (If you do not know, ask a Chamber representative or another manager in a similar company.):

2. Get information about the following:

   - ❑ Association goals, purposes, and programs:
   - ❑ Membership:
   - ❑ Available information regarding recruitment:
   - ❑ Other assistance that the representatives can suggest
   - ❑ Names and telephone numbers of others whom you should contact:

Name	Telephone Number
______________________________	______________________
______________________________	______________________
______________________________	______________________

Tip 12: Emphasize the Value of Your Employees

Managers in employer-of-choice organizations are genuinely respected by staff members. This respect, in turn, becomes the foundation for the culture of the organization that consistently emphasizes its employees.

In Tip 7, you saw how position titles empower employees. They also say a great deal about your respect for your staff members. Consider the following examples:

Common Name	Alternative Name
Secretary	Associate
Dishwasher	Steward
Sales Clerk	Sales Associate
Grass Cutter	Grounds Keeper
Maid	Room Attendant; Housekeeper
Desk Clerk	Guest Service Representative
Janitor	Facility Attendant

You can take job titles to an extreme (for example, referring to a janitor as a "sanitation engineer"). However, this is less likely to happen when you incorporate genuine concern and respect for staff members into the positions created for them.

The emphasis on employee importance goes far beyond job titles. Are you recruiting an *employee* or a *team member*? Are you recruiting someone for a *job* or a possible *career*? Are you looking for *help* or are you offering an *employment opportunity*?

Managers would do well to apply the philosophy of the Ritz-Carlton Hotel organization–the only company of its type to win the prestigious Malcolm Baldridge National Quality award (twice!). Its "employee promise" is effectively incorporated into the way everything is done by that organization:

> *"At the Ritz-Carlton, our ladies and gentlemen are the most important resource in our service commitment to our guests. By applying the principles of trust, honesty, respect, integrity, and commitment, we nurture and maximize talent to the benefit of each individual and the company.*
>
> *The Ritz-Carlton fosters a work environment where diversity is valued, quality of life is enhanced, individual aspirations are fulfilled, and the Ritz-Carlton mystique is strengthened."*

The employee promise is the basis for the Ritz-Carlton work environment and is honored by all employees. Simply put, it is "ladies and gentlemen serving ladies and gentlemen."

Walk Your Talk

List three things you will do at the time of recruitment to show applicants you value your employees:

1. ____________________
2. ____________________
3. ____________________

Talk with employees; list their ideas about what you can do during recruitment activities to show that employees are important in your organization:

1. ____________________
2. ____________________
3. ____________________

Make a personal commitment to walk your talk; recognize the value of employees to your organization's success, and emphasize that value in your recruitment activities.

Tip 13: Remember That Hourly Pay Isn't Everything

Employers of choice offer competitive compensation and benefit packages. They also provide numerous other employment advantages over their competitors:

- ❑ **Leadership quality**. Desirable employers show genuine respect for employees. Leaders provide employees with numerous opportunities to find pride and joy in their jobs.

- ❑ **Balance between work and personal lives**. Respect for employees means developing work schedules that consider employees' requests. On-call times are minimized, "emergency" call-ins occur infrequently, and unscheduled overtime hours are minimized.

- ❑ **Professional development and career opportunities are emphasized**. Managers should provide training opportunities that enable staff members to become proficient in their positions. They will then have opportunities to learn more through job rotation, cross-training, job enlargement, job enrichment, and related efforts. These activities enable staff members to become more valuable to the organization and to receive compensation and other recognition that rewards superior contributions.

- ❑ **A safe and comfortable work environment**. Employers of choice do not make work environments safe because they have to. They do not make work environments uncomfortable by design (to minimize expense) or by default (through lack of attention). Rather, they think, *What can be done to enhance the job environment?* Asking this question of current employees helps to identify ways to improve the work environment. For example, perhaps comfortable mats could be placed on the floor where employees must stand or walk for long periods of time. Or maybe the employee break room can be made more attractive to enable the staff to relax between work shifts.

Make sure you know each of the non-monetary benefits your staff members receive. Include this information in your recruitment package (see Tip 8) and mention these during interviews with applicants.

Enhance Your Workplace

List three non-monetary actions you can take to make your jobs more enjoyable; then complete the following table.

Possible Action	Why would you appreciate this?	Would your staff also appreciate this?
		❑ yes ❑ no
		❑ yes ❑ no
		❑ yes ❑ no

For each action, what must you do to implement it?

1. ______________________________

____

2. ______________________________

____

3. ______________________________

____

How can you best inform applicants that these non-monetary features are in place?

____

____

STRATEGY 2

Find the Best—General Recruitment Techniques

Tip 14: Consider Current Employees First–Promote from Within

Employers of choice hire and train employees for careers–not for jobs. Vacancies are opportunities to show employees that their organization cares about them and will reward those who excel (by promotion with higher compensation).

Consider the following potential challenges when using a promote-from-within policy:

- ❏ How is an employee selected when more than one staff member applies?
- ❏ How can a staff member continue to be motivated when a promotion or job transfer has not been granted?
- ❏ How can teamwork be encouraged when there is competition between members of the group for a promotion or transfer?

These and related questions are tough to answer; they require that objective procedures be in place to evaluate current employees for job vacancies. They also require that you be respectful, honest, and fair.

Evaluate Your Promotion Policies

Think about a position for which you expect a vacancy within the next several months, and for which one or more of your current entry-level employees may wish to apply.

Position: ____

What task or tasks must an employee in that position be able to do that an entry-level employee would not generally know how or be able to do?

Task	**How Task Is Learned** (training, on the job, and so on)	Time Required to Learn the Task

Develop a schedule to prepare potentially eligible employees for this promotion.

Employee Name	Task to Be Learned	How It Will Be Taught	Completion Date

Tip 15: Reward Current Employees for Referrals

Regardless of how you recruit workers, you incur an expense. Newspaper, magazine, and radio ads, and other recruitment tactics are expensive. You can spend those same dollars in-house by offering them to current employees who make successful employment referrals. Establish a scale that pays a specified amount if the referred employee stays 30 days, an additional amount at 90 days and, perhaps, additional payments at six and 12 months. If this sounds expensive, ask yourself, If I had no turnover for one year in a specific position, what would I save in recruiting, employee processing, training, and other costs? Why not increase your retention rate and the satisfaction level of your current employees who make referrals by giving them part of those savings? You'll gain the services of a new employee who, like his or her peer, may become a long-term member of your team.

Money can be an excellent motivator in this type of program. If it is not possible to make cash payments, consider other rewards, including special scheduling consideration, improved work assignments, and paid days off.

Employees who stay with you like your organization. They know the type of person who will be successful in it. Put this attitude and knowledge to work for you by implementing an internal referral program.

Developing an Internal Referral System

1. Consider what kind of cash payments you could make to employees who refer a successful candidate:

   $__________ after ___________ days (months)

   $__________ after ___________ days (months)

   $__________ after ___________ days (months)

2. What other, non-financial, rewards might you offer for referrals?

   ____

   ____

3. Consider how you might promote the program to your employees:

   ____

   ____

4. What might you do to increase the success of the program? (If possible, ask your employees for their ideas.)

   ____

   ____

Tip 16: Recruit Former Employees

Employees decide to leave for a variety of reasons:

- Difficulty performing the job
- Conflict(s) with co-workers or supervisors
- Work schedule problems
- Inability to secure dependable transportation
- Illness
- Family obligations

One thing certain in life is change. Children grow up and "empty nester" parents wish to return to work. The new job that an employee left for turns out to deliver less than promised. Supervisors who created conflict leave your organization and make it desirable for those who left because of them to return. Even the core requirements of a job can change, making it more attractive to a former employee.

If you track the reasons why good employees voluntarily leave (using exit interviews), you can contact them if circumstances change. Document each employee's reason for voluntarily leaving. Then, if factors change, recruit your former employees. They may be seeking permanent or temporary employment, or they may be available under certain circumstances. Make it easy for the good ones to return!

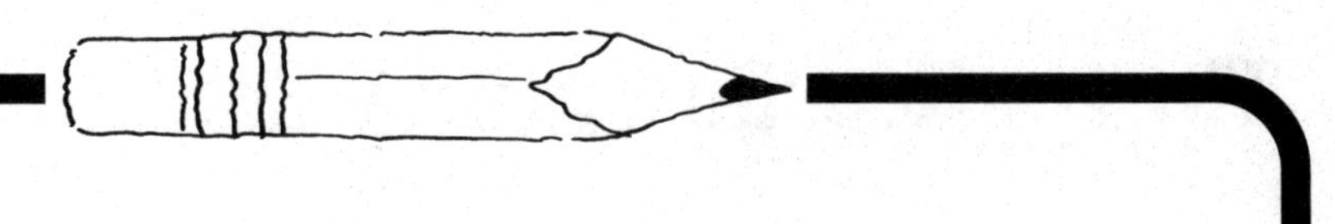

Rate Your Exit Interviewing Procedure

Recall a time when you left a job you liked. Would you have been comfortable telling your supervisor the reason you left the job?

❑ Yes ❑ No ❑ Maybe

In larger companies, exit interviews are often conducted by someone from a human resources department, which makes it easier for the departing employee to truthfully state his or her reasons for leaving.

Who conducts the exit interviews at your workplace?

____

Is this the person most appropriate for the job?

❑ Yes ❑ No ❑ Maybe

What can managers do to make valued departing employees feel comfortable during an exit interview?

____

____

____

Make copies of the following form, recording pertinent information about resigning employees during exit interviews. Put one copy in the employee's personnel file and a second copy in a special recruiting file that can be accessed as vacancies occur.

EMPLOYEES ELIGIBLE FOR REHIRE

Employee's name: ____

Address: ____

Telephone number: _____________ Email address: _______________

Name and telephone number of relative: _______________________

____

Last day of work: ____

Reason(s) for resignation: __________________________________

____

____

Comments: ____

____

____

Completed by: ____

(Name of Manager)

Tip 17: Make Employment Ads Memorable

Consider the following short ads that you might place in your local newspaper:

To which ad would you be more likely to respond? With the same few number of words, the second ad describes the type of person wanted by the business, the hospitable working environment, and opportunities for advancement.

Just because ads are short doesn't mean they can't stand out. How you describe the opportunities you offer potential employees can make a tremendous difference in the number of applicants applying for your jobs.

Each ad should strongly emphasize the positive features of your jobs that you identified earlier in this book (see Tips 5 and 6). Use features that most directly target the audience you are seeking with each ad. Consider the following two headlines for an ad placed by a golf club needing wait staff:

Employer One: *Help Wanted: Wait Staff*

Employer Two: *Avid Part-Time Golfers Needed in Our Restaurant!*

The second employer is stressing a great employee benefit; this ad is sure to attract applicants! Develop help wanted ads that tell applicants both what you are looking for and why they should join your organization.

Practice Polishing Your Company Image

Review Tips 5 and 6. Select one "best feature" from each, and in the space below, incorporate those two features in an advertisement that could be posted on a bulletin board that potential applicants might view. Keep your ad to 25 words or less, and make it memorable!

____

____

____

____

Now ask your employees for their ideas about the ad you drafted, or to brainstorm another possible ad. Use the following space to record their ideas. You might be pleasantly surprised by the high-quality, creative, and effective ads you and your staff can develop.

____

____

____

____

Tip 18: Use Current Employee Endorsements in Employment Ads

Why do we see movie stars, professional athletes, and other famous people appearing in television, billboard, and magazine ads making product endorsements? For one thing, sponsors think they will be believable, and hope that potential buyers will want to be just like them, which translates into using the product. As viewers, we often believe we can trust these celebrities more than we can trust the product manufacturers themselves.

A potential applicant for a position in your organization who reads a testimonial from a current employee might likewise reason:

- ➤ That person is just like me; if he or she thinks the job is good, maybe I will too.
- ➤ I think a person like me is more likely to be "telling the truth" about a job than is the owner or manager.
- ➤ I should check this out to see if the job is as good as it's being described by that employee.

Use the following guidelines when using current employees to endorse your organization:

- ➤ Match the employee with the type of person you are attempting to attract; if you have success with an older employee in a position, for example, use an older worker in the endorsement.
- ➤ Ask current employees to volunteer their ideas. Ask them in advance to consider an open-ended question such as "What do you like most about your job with our company?". Then, evaluate their genuine and unedited response. (Sometimes the unexpected ideas and slang words in their response produces a great recruitment message.)
- ➤ Have employees sign a legal release form that grants you permission to use their statements in advertising messages.
- ➤ Change the employee and the message frequently. The resulting "campaign" that is produced will further position your organization as an employer of choice in the community.

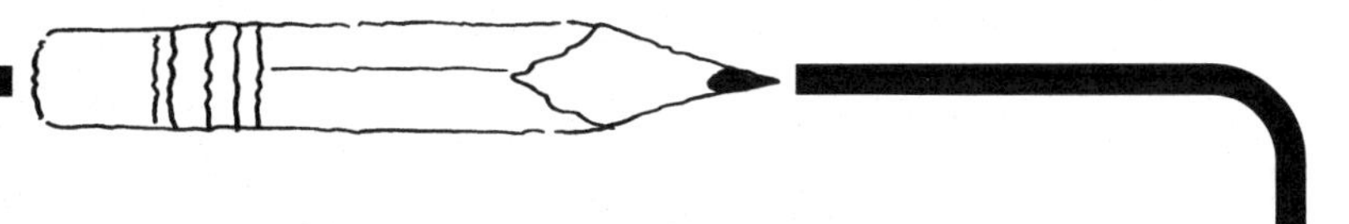

Create an Employee Endorsement Ad

1. Where could you place a brief employee endorsement about your company? (Check all that apply)

   - ❑ Help wanted ads
   - ❑ Recruitment package
   - ❑ Community bulletin boards
   - ❑ Interior signage
   - ❑ Flyers distributed at job fairs, in product purchases, and so on.
   - ❑ Company Web site
   - ❑ Company newsletter
   - ❑ Other: ______________________________

2. If you and your employees have identified the best features of your jobs and your organization (see Tips 5 and 6), provide a list of these features to employees who volunteer to make an endorsement. You could then request that they talk about, in their own words, selected features that have been identified.

3. Don't edit the message in any significant way. Correct the spelling and punctuation if needed, but allow the employee to focus on the message in his or her own way.

4. Employees can write their own endorsement, or you can give them time to think about a question (for example, "What do you like most about your job and the company?"), and record their answers yourself. Use direct quotes whenever possible; allow the employee to review and change what you have recorded before the endorsement is completed.

CONTINUED

CONTINUED

List three specific questions you could ask employees to address as they make their endorsements. Use questions that enable staff members to be creative as they describe some aspect of their job that makes them think, Wow, this is a great place to work!

Question 1: ______________________________

____

Question 2: ______________________________

____

Question 3: ______________________________

____

Tip 19: Recruit Your Customers

Your customers could be a great source of job applicants if only they knew you were looking for new team members. You want to announce that you're seeking job applicants, but you don't want customers to worry that the products or services they are receiving are inadequate because you have insufficient staff to meet their needs.

Interior signage should subtly alert customers who are potential applicants that you may be seeking employees. They might respond immediately, or they may recall your invitation to apply for a position in the future when they are actively seeking work.

Signage should be unobtrusive, not blatant. Consider placing a small sign in the dressing room of a retail clothing store or at the cash register at a video rental store. Send the right message, using tactful wording.

Here are examples of *poor* invitations to apply for a position:

⊘ Help Wanted

⊘ Looking for a Job?

Here are better examples of appropriate recruitment messages:

☺ Want to Join Our Team?

☺ Smiling Faces Always Wanted

☺ Start Your Career with Us

Be sure your recruitment package (see Tip 8) is available for anyone responding to your interior signage.

Signage will not be effective if customers observe confusion, inadequate supervision, undesirable working conditions, and other negative factors when they visit your workplace. People will only want to work for your company if they can observe that the employees, the environment, and the work situation are compatible with their perceptions of "good" employers.

Create Your Own Interior Signage

Use the following space to draft two messages (20 words or less) that you might use for interior recruitment signage. After you write the first draft, revise it in column two, ask employees for their input, and then make a final version in column three.

First Draft	Revised Draft	Final Draft

Tip 20: Provide Your Recruitment Package with Sales or Services

Tip 19 suggested that some of your customers may be potential employees. How else can you tactfully alert them about employment opportunities? Consider providing all or parts of your recruitment package with their purchases. For example, a retail clothing store could include recruitment information in the bag provided with customer purchases. Many fast-food operations incorporate recruitment and/or job application forms onto the tray liners on which food is placed. Newsletters or flyers provided with product purchases from beauty salons, or passed out with theater tickets are other examples of how you can get the word out about employment opportunities with your organization. Always ensure that your invitation to apply for work does not suggest that customers are receiving substandard products or services. You must also be careful not to offend current customers who are not in your pool of potential applicants. If this tactic might be useful in your organization with certain customers, you should consider it.

Planning a Customer Recruitment Campaign

1. Do you think some of your existing customers would like to know about employment opportunities with your business? ❑ Yes ❑ No

   If yes, what types of customers would be interested? ________________

   ____

2. What specific ideas would be helpful in implementing this strategy?

   Would you ask "target" customers if they would like information about available positions? ❑ Yes ❑ No

   With what information would you provide them–your entire recruitment package or just selected information? (If the latter, what types of information would you include?)

   ____

   ____

   Where can you place recruitment information for easiest distribution to your customers?

   ____

   ____

   On what date will you begin this recruitment method? ______________

Tip 21: Contact Your State Employment Commission

Are you aware of the services provided by your State Employment Commission (often called the *Unemployment Office*)? Many employers fail to take advantage of the free services of this agency. Your State Employment Commission can be an excellent source of job applicants, and this can be a very cost-effective recruitment tactic.

A primary purpose of this agency is to match employers with individuals who are seeking work. Whereas those looking for work often go there, those needing workers often do not. When you contact your State Employment Commission about jobs, you will be requested to supply information such as the following:

- Name, address, and telephone number of your business or organization
- A brief description of the positions you wish to fill (job title, pay range, hours available, and so on). Keep this information updated.
- A brief description of the skills and experience required for the position
- The contact person(s) for interviewing
- Established interview days and/or hours

Use the following guidelines to effectively interact with the State Employment Commission:

- Establish a direct relationship with at least one of the employment counselors; this person can become a great advocate for your jobs.
- Provide feedback. If an employee works out, let a representative know. If a new employee does not work out, let someone know this as well. Work together to find out why.
- Seek the job counselor's advice about how competitive your positions are compared with others in your industry. Factors such as pay, working conditions, and benefits can sometimes best be evaluated by an individual (the counselor) who sees the offerings of many employers.

Use Your Local Government Agency

1. What is the telephone number of your State Employment Commission? (Note that the exact name of this agency varies from state to state. Consult your local telephone directory.): ______________________________

2. What is the name of the individual(s) with whom you spoke?

____

3. What general procedures must you follow to file job openings with the agency?

____

____

____

____

4. What other information can the agency provide to assist you with your recruitment efforts?

____

____

____

5. Are there other state or local government agencies that can provide recruitment assistance? ❑ Yes ❑ No

If yes, list the names and telephone numbers of these agencies:

Agency Name	Telephone Number
______________________	______________
______________________	______________
______________________	______________
______________________	______________

Tip 22: Be Creative in Where You Look

Expand your pool of potential applicants by promoting your jobs in the places where potential workers are likely to see them. If teens are a likely source of job applicants, advertise your openings in school newspapers, in the printed programs for sporting events, plays, or concerts, and in popular local hangouts. The costs are low and your message is aimed for its intended audience.

If older workers are a potential applicant source, consider locations where they will likely learn about your needs. Examples include newsletters and bulletin boards of retirement communities, supermarkets, golf courses, fraternal organizations, garden clubs, libraries, and museums.

Remember that your goal is to consistently get your message out in a way that is memorable and cost-effective. When posting position openings, include information about *why* working with your organization makes good sense for your intended audience (refer to Tips 5 and 6).

Where Do Your Likely Candidates Hang Out?

Consider employees who have been successful in your organization. List several places where similar people are likely to see employment information. Write down potential methods of communicating with them (for example, ads, flyers, bulletin board notices, and so on). Post your position vacancies in at least five places where you have never before recruited.

Potential Applicant Location	Potential Advertising Method
1. ____________________	____________________
2. ____________________	____________________
3. ____________________	____________________
4. ____________________	____________________
5. ____________________	____________________

Don't forget that your current employees are a good source of information when implementing this strategy.

Tip 23: Add an Employment Section to Your Organization's Web Site

Today, organizations of all types are adding an employment opportunities section to their home page on the World Wide Web. Millions of individuals, including teenagers and seniors, regularly use the Internet as a job-seeking tool. If your business or organization already has a Web site, it can serve as a significant source of potential applicants, especially if it includes an "employment opportunities" section designed to proactively recruit for your positions.

The capability to apply for a position online may significantly "stack the deck" in your favor when job seekers are deciding where they should focus their time and energy. As more businesses begin using this recruitment method, those that do not will be left behind.

If you do not currently have a Web site and find the idea of creating one daunting, numerous resources are available to help you get started. Talk to other computer-savvy business owners, visit your local library or bookstore, or search the Internet itself. If you still feel intimidated, consult a telephone directory or get a referral for the name of someone who designs Web sites for a fee. Designing Web sites is a big business, and for a good reason: Huge numbers of potential employees are out there "surfing the Web" right now.

Evaluate Your "Electronic Options"

Many organizations make use of online recruiting. Check out the following Web sites. Review their *employment or career opportunity* sections to discover ideas that may be relevant to your business. Carefully consider adding this important component to your organization's Web site.

- ❑ Boeing Corporation: www.boeing.com
- ❑ NCR: www.ncr.com
- ❑ Disney: www.disney.go.com/disneycareers
- ❑ Meijer Stores Limited: www.meijer.com
- ❑ Northwest Airlines: www.nwa.com/corpinfo/career

In addition, review the Web sites of your competitors and other businesses in your community. When looking at Web sites, note the features that may be useful to your organization.

Company	Web Site Address	Special Features in the Employment/Careers Section

If you don't currently have a Web site and would like to create one, list the names and telephone numbers of three people who could help you get started:

Name	**Telephone Number**
______________________	______________________
______________________	______________________
______________________	______________________

Tip 24: Include an "Employment Center" on a Public Bulletin Board

Many organizations offer a public bulletin board. Employees (and sometimes customers) may post information about a wide variety of topics, including the following:

- ➤ Community events
- ➤ Items for sale
- ➤ Upcoming product releases (such as new videos)
- ➤ Coupons from recent newspapers or flyers (which others may use)
- ➤ Public governmental notices
- ➤ Advertisements from schools and community organizations

You can include an attractive "Employment Center" feature in your bulletin board. It could invite readers to apply for open positions with your organization, and could include components of your recruitment package.

You might be surprised by the degree to which a relatively small "Employment Center" section (which consumes only a little of your bulletin board's available space) can be a very effective recruitment tactic; give it a try!

Create an Employment Center

Visit pharmacies or grocery stores, recreational centers, social clubs, and other businesses in your community. Review the bulletin boards that they offer for public use and note whether they offer employment materials about their own organization on them.

1. What are some ideas that you can adapt and improve? ______________

____

____

2. What design components can you incorporate into your own Employment Center?

____

____

3. What else must be done before you can begin offering an Employment Center on your bulletin board? (Use the following space to outline your planning activities.)

Activity	Assigned To	Completion Date

4. Choose a date by which you plan to have an Employment Center component on your bulletin board: ______________________________

Tip 25: Participate in Community Events and Programs

Many communities offer ethnic festivals, holiday special celebration events, community-wide recognition programs, activities sponsored by community service organizations, and so on. You can become involved in events to help fulfill your role as an "active citizen." Your participation can also enhance your reputation as an employer of choice. When managers evaluate participation alternatives (which are frequently numerous), they often evaluate costs incurred only relative to potential future customer sales. You should, however, also consider costs relative to an event's recruitment potential. Participating in these events may enable you to alert many potential applicants about employment opportunities. You can be undertaking recruiting efforts at the same time you are supporting worthwhile community causes. You'll likely note that these events attract committed, high-quality staff with strong values. This is especially true for events related to community service, education, and other socially responsible causes. Therefore, the quality of applicants generated from these events is likely to be high.

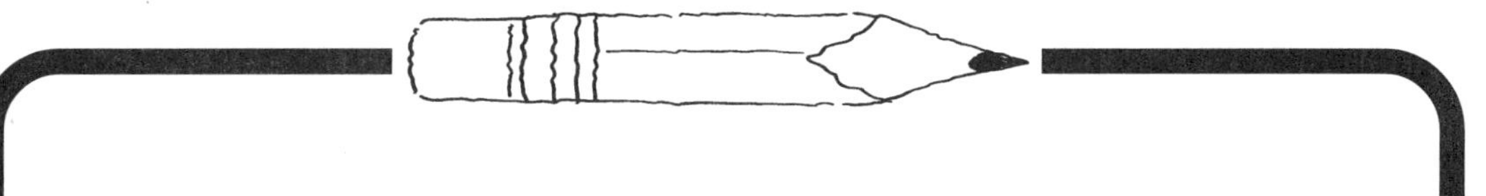

Making the "Community Connection"

Think about community festivals, celebrations, and other events in which you have participated:

1. In retrospect, is it likely that you were in contact with many potential job applicants?

   ❑ Yes ❑ No

2. If yes, did you talk about and/or distribute recruitment package materials?

   ❑ Yes ❑ No

   Did your efforts yield good job applicants?

   ❑ Yes ❑ No

   Could you have done a more effective job of recruiting at these events?

   ❑ Yes ❑ No

   If yes, what might you do to increase your effectiveness? ____________

   ____

   ____

   ____

3. What events do you plan to attend within the next 12 months?

Name of Event	Date(s)	Contact Person(s)

STRATEGY **3**

Develop "Youth Appeal"

Tip 26: Evaluate Your Dress Code

Managers in all types of businesses wrestle with the issue of dress codes. Dress code requirements should not be arbitrary; they should be rational and defensible. Today, even conservative bankers and Wall Street executives have adopted "casual Fridays," acknowledging the trend toward more informal and individual-oriented business attire.

Clothing worn by your staff must be appropriate to the job. Loose clothing may be a safety hazard when one works around machinery. Hard-toed shoes may be essential for some jobs. Flashy jewelry may be deemed inappropriate in some customer contact positions.

There are times when a specific costume or uniform may be important (to carry out a specific theme in a restaurant, for example). In other instances, however, uniforms may pose a hindrance to effective recruiting. If you require a specific uniform, make sure that there is a good reason for it (not "we've always required it."). In addition, make sure that it reflects current styles in street wear as much as possible. At the very least, neither young employees nor older employees should feel that the uniform is foolish or humiliating in any way.

Revisit Your Dress Code Policy

1. If your organization requires any type of uniform, ask at least three employees what they think of the uniform.

2. If they dislike the current uniform or think it hinders the effective recruitment of potential employees, ask for suggestions about how to make the uniform more attractive or contemporary.

Include information about your uniform and dress code requirements, if any, in your employee handbook and provide this information during new employee orientation. If no specific uniform is required or if there is a requirement that is highly popular with most workers, consider adding this "benefit" to your recruitment brochure.

Tip 27: Use the Buddy System

For many young workers, where their friends work has a powerful influence on where they themselves work or want to work. If your workplace employs enough staff to allow it, consider advertising for and then hiring "work buddies."

Encourage and hire friends who apply for jobs at about the same time. Schedule them for the same days and the same shifts. If possible, schedule them to work in the same department or area of your organization; and give them the same days off. A system such as this can increase their attendance as well as your retention rate.

While this approach might be considered unconventional by many persons, to effectively compete against other businesses in the labor market, you need to be creative, and sometimes unconventional. If you are successful at hiring friends, you will, at the same time, double your effectiveness in filling critical entry-level position vacancies!

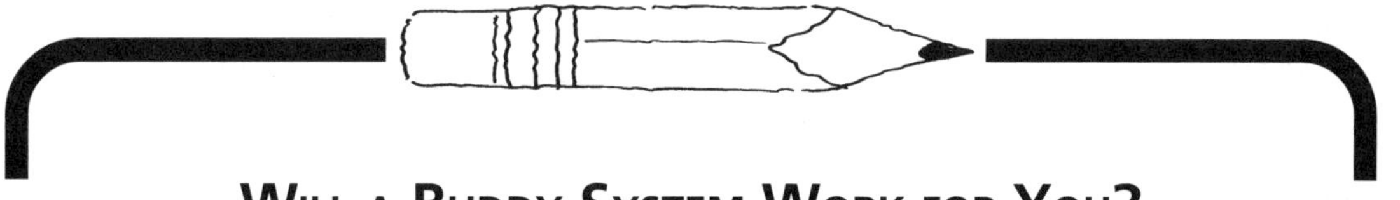

Will a Buddy System Work for You?

Many fitness experts suggest that people are more likely to begin and continue a serious exercise program if they have an "exercise buddy" who works out with them.

1. What similarities do you see between an exercise program and the first jobs taken by younger workers?

___

___

2. In what positions and departments might a buddy system be successful?

Position	Department

3. If you think a buddy system would work at your company, how and when will you implement this recruitment tactic?

___

___

___

Tip 28: Sponsor Work-Study Programs

Many organizations benefit from participating in work-study programs with their local high schools and/or post-secondary schools. (These programs are also referred to as internships, apprenticeships, and externships.) Becoming a partner in a program such as this can help in your efforts to become known as an employer of choice.

Contact local school officials, vocational education departments, and guidance counselors (see Tip 30). Invite one or more school representatives to visit your organization and learn how you might help with their students' education in the "real world" of your business. A successful program can yield several advantages:

- You obtain assistance for work that needs to be done.
- You can check out potential employees to whom you might offer part- or full-time work now or after graduation.
- Potential employees can check out you and your organization; this way, there's less likely to be "surprises" after they begin work, which can lead to rapid turnover.
- The teacher/coordinator/counselor visiting your organization will likely be impressed and become an active recruiter for your organization in his or her work-study activities
- The school representatives may seek part-time, seasonal, summer, or other employment opportunities with you.

CREATE A WORK-STUDY PROGRAM

If you think a work-study program is feasible at your workplace, contact your local school and arrange to meet with a teacher or coordinator to dicuss your work-study program ideas. Prepare for that meeting by answering these questions:

1. What job(s) do you have that might be available for work-study students?

____

____

2. How many **hours** weekly could the students work in your positions?

____

3. How many **students** per week could be involved in a work-study program?

____

4. How, if at all, would current jobs need to be modified to meet the needs of work-study students?

____

____

5. As an employer, what do you see as your responsibilities in a successful work-study effort?

____

____

Tip 29: Invite Classes for Tours and Discussions

Educators frequently look for ways to bring the "real world" into their classrooms. One tactic involves field trips. You can help your community's schools and students, and yourself, by accommodating instructors with visits to your workplace.

While a "tour" in a traditional sense (students in small groups being shown different workstations) may be useful, you have many alternatives. Students may view non-public spaces such as receiving and storage areas. They may be given a "hands-on" opportunity to use an electronic cash register and/or credit card authorization equipment.

During the tour, those in attendance can be given basic information about your organization, including its recruitment package (see Tip 8). You can discuss "a day in the life of" a typical current employee, or invite an employee to share interesting anecdotes about his or her position.

Many students are looking for a part-time position during school, and perhaps full-time work during non-school periods. Exposure to your organization during field trips, your recruitment package, and encouragement to apply for a position may yield additional staff members for you.

Develop a Guided Student Tour

Consider involving your entry-level employees in the development of a student tour. After all, these are the types of applicants you are targeting in your recruitment efforts.

1. Describe what *you* think students on a field trip could learn by visiting your organization:

   ____

   ____

2. Now ask some of your entry-level staff what they think students could learn:

   ____

   ____

Contacts for Local Schools

High School

Name ____

Title __________________ Telephone Number ____________

Relevant Classes __________________________________

Appointment Date _________________________________

Vocational School

Name ____

Title __________________ Telephone Number ____________

Relevant Classes __________________________________

Appointment Date _________________________________

Community/Junior College

Name ____

Title __________________ Telephone Number ____________

Relevant Classes __________________________________

Appointment Date _________________________________

College/University

Name ____

Title __________________ Telephone Number ____________

Relevant Classes __________________________________

Appointment Date _________________________________

Tip 30: Meet with School Guidance Counselors

Vocational counselors sometimes hold stereotypes that influence the perceptions and attitudes driving their recommendations. Counselors that "know" that fast-food establishments only offer hot, noisy, and greasy environments may view these organizations differently after a behind-the-scenes visit. If you offer class tours (see Tip 29) be sure to invite the guidance counselor(s) to accompany the students.

Alternatively, make a specific and personal invitation for the counselor(s) to visit your workplace at a mutually convenient time. This visit can help ensure that the counselor forms a positive impression of your industry and organization. You can create a powerful ally by enlisting the support of a popular, well-respected guidance counselor.

Use the checklist on the next page to make the most of your visit with the school guidance counselor.

School Guidance Counselor Checklist

Name of counselor: ______________ Telephone Number: __________

Significant points to make in invitations (for example, exciting positions leading to rewarding careers, skills the students will be taught, and so on):

- ❑ ____
- ❑ ____
- ❑ ____

Major points to cover during counselor's visit:

- ❑ Organization's mission
- ❑ Basic demographic data about your organization and your industry
- ❑ Tour of operations
- ❑ Significant challenges
- ❑ Ways that student employees can help the organization
- ❑ Ways that the organization can help student employees
- ❑ Basic career information
- ❑ Other information: ____________________________________

Materials to give counselor:

- ❑ Recruitment package to keep on file
- ❑ Extra copies of recruitment package for distribution
- ❑ Other: ____

Tip 31: "Mobilize" Your Message!

One challenge in recruiting young people is discovering creative ways to alert them to job and career opportunities with you. Consider using flyers on cars parked in school parking lots, shopping mall parking lots, and other public parking areas frequented by students.

What should your flyer say? The same strategies used by billboard designers are applicable here: Keep the message fun, short, and to the point; and stress the job's advantages to the student reader (flexible hours, for example).

It is hoped that you already have something designed, which you are using in your recruitment package (see Tip 8). If so, this flyer can be duplicated for distribution. If a flyer is not currently available, some creative effort will be necessary (see the following activity).

Try marking your flyers with a code that indicates which location they came from. For example, distribute to the school parking lot a version of the flyer marked with "SPL." When students call to inquire about your workplace, you can ask them to identify the code on their flyer. This will help you evaluate the effectiveness of various locations.

Will a flyer work? Like all the tips in this book, you'll need to try it, perhaps modify it, and decide whether it is effective in attracting suitable applicants.

Your "Parking Lot" Strategy

1. Do you currently have a brochure or flyer that clearly (and briefly) stresses the benefits and best features of your organization and its jobs (see Tips 5 and 6)?

   ❑ Yes ❑ No

2. If yes, can the brochure be used in its current form as a flyer for distribution?

   ❑ Yes ❑ No

3. If no, what changes must be made?

4. Is contact information available? (This can include your business location, the name of the person to contact, and times to call.)

   ❑ Yes ❑ No (If you answer no, refer to Question 5)

5. If a flyer is not currently available, you can design one. In the following space, describe the best features of your jobs and your organization. Refer to the activities for Tips 5 and 6 for this information. In short, you are describing why a student would want to work for you.

Best Features of Job	Best Features of Organization
______________________	______________________
______________________	______________________
______________________	______________________

6. What specific contact information should you include?

____

____

____

7. Who can help design the flyer? (Be sure to ask student employees for their input, because they represent the pool of potential applicants you are attempting to attract with this strategy.)

____

8. What school(s) will be targeted for the distribution?

____

____

____

9. When will the flyer be distributed? ______________________

10. Who will distribute the flyer? ______________________

STRATEGY **4**

Foster Workplace Diversity

Tip 32: Celebrate Diversity

Effective recruitment means ensuring that all qualified or potentially qualified applicants know about you and the jobs or career opportunities you offer. There is no advantage to *reducing* the pool of potentially eligible applicants. A wide range of federal, state, and local laws prohibit employment discrimination on the basis of age, sex, race, national origin, disability, creed, and religion. Employers of choice understand that this legislation represents not only the *legal* thing to do, but also the *right* and the best thing to do.

Many of the tips in this book have emphasized a "win-win" aspect to recruitment tactics. The applicants who are employed win because they are affiliated with an employer of choice that treats staff members with genuine respect. The employer wins because a diverse staff results in a dynamic, creative workplace, and one in which the different perspectives and backgrounds are likely to reflect the customer base.

What are the *disadvantages* to a culturally diverse work force? There are none. Once you identify the core requirements of your jobs (see Tip 4), recruit and hire anyone who can do or learn to do those jobs. Any individual who can make a positive contribution to your workplace is an individual you want to hire and retain.

The Benefits of a Diverse Workforce

How can a diverse workforce help in your efforts to be an employer of choice?

____

Describe a specific way in which a diverse workforce can benefit your organization:

____

Describe two examples of successes you (or your organization) have had as a result of cultural diversity:

Example 1: ______________________________________

____

____

Example 2: ______________________________________

____

____

Tip 33: Remember Your BOQs!

Bona fide occupational qualifications (BOQs) are the law of the land, and they make good recruitment sense. A BOQ is a job qualification that has been established in good faith and fairness, one that is necessary to safely or adequately perform the job.

To establish a bona fide occupational qualification, you must prove that some employees would not be able to perform the job safely or adequately, and that the BOQ is reasonably necessary. The following items are examples of qualifications that may be appropriate for various jobs:

- Attributes such as the ability to lift a specific amount of weight
- Level of education reached
- Certifications
- Registrations
- Licensing
- Language skills
- Knowledge of equipment operation
- Previous experience
- Minimum age requirements (such as for serving alcohol or working certain hours)

VERIFYING YOUR BOQs

Now think about a position for which you do occasional (or more frequent!) recruiting.

Position Title: ____

1. What are the core requirements of this position? List the essential elements below:

   ______________________ ______________________

   ______________________ ______________________

   ______________________ ______________________

2. How might you modify the essential elements described above to accommodate the following, if possible:

   ❑ An employee confined to a wheelchair ____________________

   ____

   ❑ An employee who doesn't speak fluent English ______________

   ____

   ❑ An employee who is hearing impaired____________________

   ____

   ❑ An employee who is visually impaired ____________________

   ____

   ❑ An employee with limited limb mobility ___________________

   ____

Tip 34: Consider Lateral Job Changes

You may find it beneficial to consider current employees for positions that do not involve promotion but need to be filled. For example, it may be more difficult to fill the position of cashier than that of stock clerk in a grocery store. It may be more difficult to find a skilled bartender than a dining room server for a restaurant. If current employees can be moved to the more difficult-to-fill positions, your recruitment efforts (for the less difficult to fill position) become easier.

An employee can be "groomed" for these alternate positions. Of course, the employee must first be proficient in the position for which he or she was hired. Then, to reduce boredom and to motivate the employee ("Wow, my boss recognizes my abilities and sees that I can do other things!"), additional on-the-job learning can occur. You can facilitate this learning in several ways:

Job rotation

Sometimes (during slow work shifts, for example), an employee working in a specific position may not be needed. Give this employee the opportunity to closely observe another job being performed, and to begin to perform simple work tasks routinely done by employees in another position.

Job enlargement

You can periodically assign employees to do one or more tasks that are not part of the job for which they have been hired. (Be sure to schedule work assignments so that affected employees are not required to do all their work plus additional tasks as well.) Over time, these employees can learn how to do many, if not all, of the tasks required by the other position.

Cross-training

Successful employees may be given opportunities to train for other positions on an "as time is available" basis.

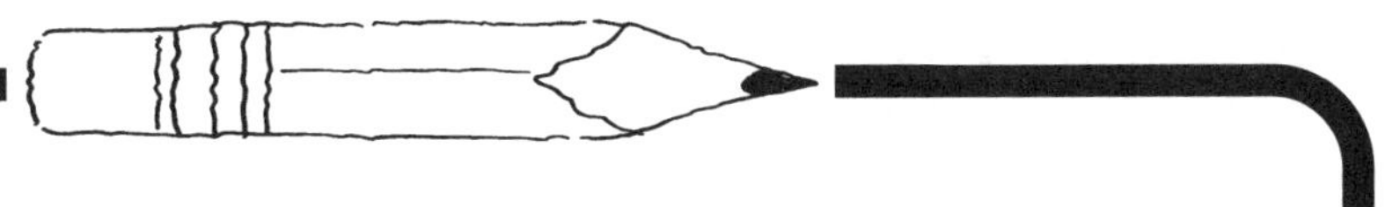

Make a Plan for Employee Development

Think of an outstanding employee who does especially well in a specific entry-level position. Now consider another position involving different types of knowledge and skills for which recruitment is more difficult. Can you envision retraining the current employee for this position?

1. What basic elements in the latter (more difficult-to-recruit) position might be learned by the high-performing employee?

____

____

2. Why might the high-performing employee want to learn this information or acquire these skills?

____

____

3. What would be the best way to train this high-performing employee for the other position?

____

____

4. How long would it take for the current employee to become proficient in these new tasks?

____

____

5. Describe what aspects of the new position might make it attractive to the high-performing employee:

____

____

Tip 35: SOS! (Seek Out Seniors)

Workers aged 55 to 64 are the fastest growing segment of the labor market. They can be of tremendous value in helping to fill your entry-level positions if you understand and respond to their reason(s) for working.

Consider the following facts about older workers:

- They miss fewer days of work, on average, due to illness than do their younger counterparts.
- They require less training in most jobs.
- They are the fastest growing group of Internet users, and adapt well to changing technology
- They stay with their employers as long as the average worker does.
- They are noted, as a group, for their loyalty and dedication.

Older persons work for most of the same reasons anyone works. Many are retired and want to supplement their income. Others enjoy the stimulation of work and the social aspects. Still others welcome the opportunity to learn new skills.

You may need to be more flexible in order to maximize your use of older workers. If you can be, they are likely to respond favorably to your recruitment efforts.

Evaluate Your Attitude About Employing Seniors

Consider the jobs in your company currently filled by entry-level workers. Are there any that could not successfully (or legally) be done by a *younger* worker? Now consider your jobs again. Are there any that could not successfully be done by a worker aged 55 or older?

1. If yes, identify the job(s) and the age constraints:

   ______________________ ______________________

   ______________________ ______________________

2. How could you modify these jobs to make them more attractive to older workers? (For example, can work areas be redesigned? Can carts be used to transport heavy items? Can lighting be improved?)

   ____

   ____

3. Make sure your current older workers know about your efforts to recruit others in their age group, and ask them for their recruitment ideas. Record their suggestions here:

   ______________________ ______________________

   ______________________ ______________________

   ______________________ ______________________

Tip 36: Consider Applicants in Career Transition

Many employers recognize that the knowledge and job skills necessary for entry-level positions can be taught; what's truly important is an employee's *attitude.* Individuals who are currently without a job but who have previous job experience are prime candidates for your recruitment efforts. Some creativity and effort are necessary to identify sources of these potential staff members. The rewards–a new pool of potential applicants–may more than offset the costs incurred to recruit these persons.

On the following page are some suggestions for where you can look to find these potential applicants in transition. Contact these sources, ask if you can submit copies of your recruitment package (see Tip 8), and get to know a contact person at each organization. This will probably require an ongoing relationship built over time. If recruitment is an integral part of your own responsibilities, this is time well spent.

Sources for Potential Applicants

❑ **Outplacement organizations** (see "Outplacement Consultants" in your telephone directory)

Contact Name ______________________________

Telephone Number ______________________________

Conversation Notes: ______________________________

❑ **Vocational Schools**

Contact Name ______________________________

Telephone Number ______________________________

Conversation Notes: ______________________________

❑ **Temporary placement agencies** (see "Employment Agencies" and/or "Employment Service" listings in your telephone directory)

Contact Name ______________________________

Telephone Number ______________________________

Conversation Notes: ______________________________

❑ **Business Associations**

Contact Name ______________________________

Telephone Number ______________________________

Conversation Notes: ______________________________

❑ **Fraternal Organizations**

Contact Name ______________________________

Telephone Number ______________________________

Conversation Notes: ______________________________

Tip 37: Seek Legal Immigrants

Newly arrived immigrants often have a strong work ethic and want to show their employers that they can be successful. They likely face many challenges as they adapt to their new living and work environments, and they often become very loyal to their newfound friends, neighbors, and employers, among others. As discussed in Tip 32, employing qualified individuals from diverse backgrounds creates a rich, cosmopolitan workplace that fosters cooperation and often reflects a similarly diverse customer base.

Work through the following activity to begin your efforts to identify sources of applicants who are legal immigrants.

Increase the Diversity of Your Workplace

❑ Local churches, synagogues, and other places of worship often sponsor and/or work with immigrant groups. Contact the head of such groups in your community to ask for assistance in identifying immigrants who may be looking for work opportunities.

Name of Groups to Contact	Telephone Number
______________________	______________________
______________________	______________________
______________________	______________________

❑ English as a second language (ESL) is often taught by local high schools and/or community colleges. Teachers of these programs may be able to refer qualified applicants and/or distribute recruitment packages (see Tip 8) for you. If possible, create a simple flyer in the language of the group you are targeting. Ideally, create a flyer with the same information in both languages!

School Officials to Contact	Telephone Number
______________________	______________________
______________________	______________________
______________________	______________________

❑ State social service agencies may maintain a job listing service and/or might provide other information to help you contact state affiliates serving these constituencies.

Name	Telephone Number
______________________	______________________
______________________	______________________
______________________	______________________

MORE

MORE

- ❑ Identify local ethnic support groups (for example, clubs or meetings attended by individuals from specific areas, or with specific interests in ethnic and/or religious issues).

- ❑ Contact other local businesses that hire significant numbers of immigrants. Some organizations prohibit the employment of relatives. For example, husbands and wives, or parents and children may not be allowed to work for the same company. If this is the case, you may be able to recruit relatives of the employees working for these organizations.

S T R A T E G Y **5**

Screen to Ensure Success

Tip 38: Make Yourself Available

Okay! You have done a good job getting the word out about the opportunities you offer employees. Now, someone who is seeking a job has entered the front door of your workplace unannounced. In a perfect world, applicants would only stop in at a time when you could properly greet, screen, and then possibly interview them. Of course, that rarely happens! Potential employees can arrive anytime, and that time is often when you are very busy. If your response in this case is, "Please come back at a time that is more convenient for me," you may lose the opportunity to hire a perfect applicant.

Don't let this happen. When potential employees arrive at your place of business, do everything you can to make time to greet them. Remember that this may be their first impression of you and your organization. Make the meeting a genuinely friendly and unhurried one. At the least, you can give them a recruitment package (see Tip 8). If practical, ask them to remain and review it until you have time to speak with them. (Of course, during this time, they will be watching you and their prospective peers "in action." What they see will likely have a significant influence on their continued interest in your organization!) If you can't take time to speak with a prospective applicant, obtain a telephone number and call back as soon as possible. Be proactive; don't ask the potential applicant to contact you a second time. Then, preferably, contact the prospective employee before the end of the day to arrange a meeting time.

Realistically, no manager or owner can always be available during business hours. Potential employees can arrive at any time, however. For the activity on the next page, identify the employee(s) who should meet with an applicant wishing to apply for work when you are not available.

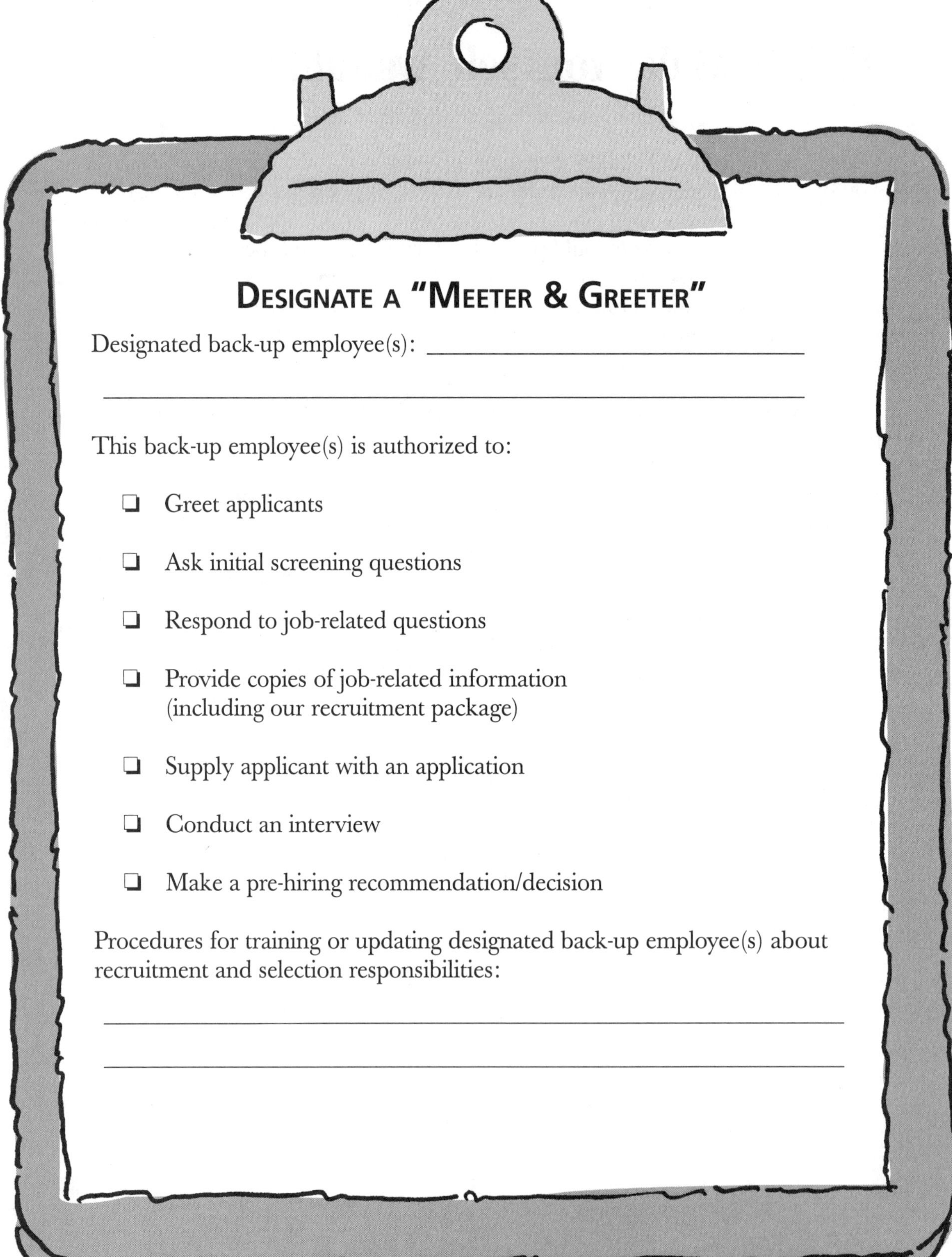

Designate a "Meeter & Greeter"

Designated back-up employee(s): ______________________________

____

This back-up employee(s) is authorized to:

❑ Greet applicants

❑ Ask initial screening questions

❑ Respond to job-related questions

❑ Provide copies of job-related information (including our recruitment package)

❑ Supply applicant with an application

❑ Conduct an interview

❑ Make a pre-hiring recommendation/decision

Procedures for training or updating designated back-up employee(s) about recruitment and selection responsibilities:

____

____

Tip 39: Conduct a Two-Minute Screening

Managers and owners know that applicants can appear at any time and ask, "Are you hiring?" The answer may be yes, but you also know that not everyone who is seeking work with you is a desirable candidate.

You can save yourself and the potential applicant time by doing an initial screening *before* the applicant completes an application and before you conduct an interview.

Whether an applicant arrives in person or calls on the telephone, you can conduct a brief and friendly pre-interview screening by asking the following questions:

> *"What type of work (job) are you seeking?"*
>
> *"Are you familiar with the basic requirements of the position we have available?"*
>
> *"Are you available to work on the days and at the times we need you?"*
>
> *"Do you understand the range of pay associated with the job(s)?"*
>
> *"Are you currently working?"*

Include any additional questions that are relevant to you or your particular operation and that will address the primary objective of the pre-screening: to separate the serious candidate from his or her not-so-serious counterpart.

Screen Out Misconceptions About the Position

Take a minute to think about two positions you offer and the candidates that have applied for them in the past. As you interviewed these candidates, what were the two biggest misconceptions they had about these positions? What questions could you ask in a pre-interview screening to address these issues?

Example

Job: Salesperson

Misconception: that compensation is based on a fixed annual salary

Question that will clarify: "Are you aware that this position pays on a commission basis?"

Job 1:

Misconception 1:____

Question that will clarify: ________________________________

Misconception 2:____

Question that will clarify: ________________________________

Job 2:

Misconception 1:____

Question that will clarify: ________________________________

Misconception 2:____

Question that will clarify: ________________________________

Tip 40: Provide a Short Tour of Your Workplace

You can increase your competitive recruitment advantage by turning a potential employee's first on-site visit into a positive and friendly experience. You can easily achieve this by doing the following:

- ➤ Provide a guided tour that enables potential employees to familiarize themselves with your workplace.
- ➤ Introduce the potential employee to your friendly and professional staff during your tour.
- ➤ Point out the area(s) where they will be working, if hired, and what they will be doing in the area(s).
- ➤ Emphasize the positive features of your jobs and your organization. (Refer to the "best features" that you defined in Tips 5 and 6.)

Your workplace provides an excellent opportunity to "sell" your organization as a good employment choice. It should be clean and safe, and provide an environment that says "Welcome" to prospective and new employees. If it is, you will likely have little trouble convincing prospective employees that their future with you will be a good one.

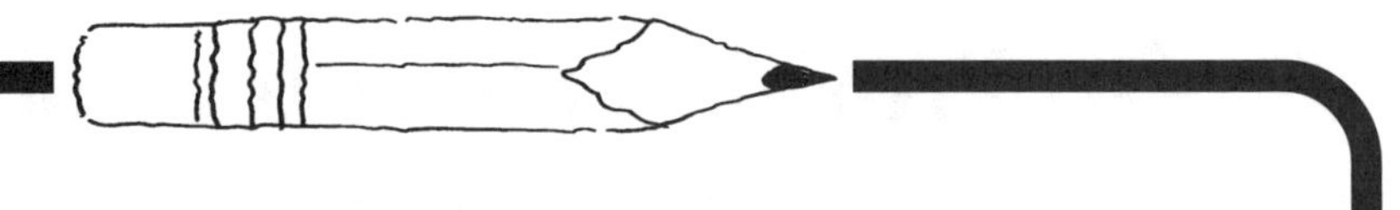

Promote Your Workplace

Pretend you are entering your workplace for the first time or recall the first time you visited your workplace. What do you first notice when you enter the work environment?

Describe three of the physical work areas and/or work activities that interested you the most.

1. ______________________________

2. ______________________________

3. ______________________________

Are these still aspects of the company that you would feature on tours of your organization that you give to prospective applicants?

❑ Yes ❑ No

What things did staff members say or do to make you feel welcome?

____

____

What current staff member(s) do you think would make the best impression(s) on a new employee if they were present when a tour was being given and why?

______________________________	______________________________
(Name)	(Name)
______________________________	______________________________
______________________________	______________________________

If possible, be sure to introduce the prospective applicant to these staff members during your tours.

Tip 41: Use a Legal Application Form

Numerous federal, state, and local laws and regulations address employment discrimination issues relating to sex, age, medical conditions, sexual orientation, race, national origin, disability, or religious creed.

Many businesses include job applications in their basic recruitment materials, including their recruitment package (see Tip 8). However, it is important (and legally necessary!) that these applications request only information that enables you to evaluate an applicant's eligibility for a position.

Information that *can* be requested	Information that *cannot* be requested
✓ Name	⊘ Marital status
✓ Address	⊘ Height
✓ Physical attributes necessary to complete the duties of the job, such as the ability to lift a specific amount of weight	⊘ Weight
✓ Education	⊘ Race
✓ Certifications	⊘ Maiden name
✓ Registrations	⊘ Country of origin
✓ Licensing	⊘ Medical history
✓ Language skills (if required for performance of the job)	⊘ Treatment for drug abuse
✓ Knowledge of equipment operation	⊘ Physical defects
✓ Previous experience	
✓ Minimum age requirements (for serving alcohol or working certain hours)	

Review Your Employment Application

Compare the application form currently used by your organization with the sample application that follows.

1. Does it appear to contain requests for information applicable to any of the topics noted above that are (or may be) in violation of discrimination laws?

   ❑ Yes ❑ No

   If yes, what is the specific information being requested? ____________

   ____

   Note: If you find elements in potential violation of discrimination laws, bring this to the attention of your manager or your human resources department.

2. As you carefully review your application form, do you notice other "nice-to-know" information that does not really help determine an applicant's eligibility for a position? If so, what information have you identified?

   ____

   ____

   ____

   This information should also be brought to the attention of your manager or the human resources department. Remember that your application forms should help to identify the widest–not the narrowest–range of potentially valuable applicants.

SAMPLE APPLICATION

Print or Type Clearly

Last Name First Middle	Position(s) Desired
Street Address	Wage/Salary Desired Date Available for Work
City State Zip	Social Security Number
Home Phone Work Phone	Are You Presently Employed? Yes No May We Contact Your Present Employer? Yes No
To verify previous employment, please indicate if you have worked under another name. Yes No If yes, other name used:	

EMPLOYMENT RECORD

List your previous experience, beginning with your most recent position. (Include military experience as a job)

Employer 1 (Area Code) Phone Number	Employer 2 (Area Code) Phone Number
Address City, State, Zip Code	Address City, State, Zip Code
Starting Position Starting Salary	Starting Position Starting Salary
Last Position Final Salary	Last Position Final Salary
Dates Employed Immediate Supervisor	Dates Employed Immediate Supervisor
Duties	Duties
Reason for Leaving	Reason for Leaving

EDUCATION AND SKILLS

School	Location	Graduation Date	Major
High School			
College			
Additional Training			

MORE

MORE

<table>
<tr><td colspan="2">Which languages do you speak fluently?</td></tr>
<tr><td colspan="2">If Job Related: Typing Speed ____________WPM Other business machines operated:______________</td></tr>
<tr><td colspan="2">Are there any hours, shifts, or days of the week that you cannot work? Please specify.</td></tr>
<tr><td colspan="2">I am able to work (check the following) FT PT On-Call Evenings Overnight Weekends Holidays Overtime</td></tr>
<tr><td>Do you have relatives or acquaintances working here? Yes No
If yes, please indicate their name and relationship.</td><td>Have you ever been convicted of a felony?
Yes No If yes, please indicate dates and details: ________________________________
____

Do you have any felony charges pending against you? Yes No ________________
Conviction of a felony will not necessarily disqualify you from employment</td></tr>
<tr><td>Are you under age 18?
Yes No</td><td>Are you authorized to work in the United States?
Yes No</td></tr>
<tr><td colspan="2">Can you perform the essential functions of the job for which you are applying with or without accommodation? Please explain.
____
____</td></tr>
</table>

PERSONAL REFERENCES (Not employers or relatives)

Name	Position and Company	Current Address	Telephone

Certification and Signature – Please Read Carefully

I declare that my answers to the questions on this application are true, and I give (company) the right to investigate all references and information given. I agree that any false statement or misrepresentation on this application will be cause for refusal to hire or immediate dismissal.

I agree that my employment will be considered "at will" and may be terminated by this company at any time without liability for wages or salary except for such as may have been earned at the date of such termination.

I understand that (company) is a drug-free workplace and has a policy against drug and alcohol use and reserves the right to screen applicants and test for cause.

I acknowledge that if I need reasonable accommodation in either the application process or employment, I should bring the request to the attention of ____________.

I authorize you to make such legal investigations and inquiries of my personal employment, criminal history, driving record, and other job-related matters as may be necessary in determining an employment decision. I hereby release employers, school, or persons from all liability in responding to inquiries in connection with my application.

I understand that an offer of employment and my continued employment are contingent upon satisfactory proof of my authorization to work in the United States of America.

Applicant's signature: ____Date _______

Tip 42: Conduct a Meaningful Interview

How would you feel if you were being interviewed for a position and the person conducting the interview:

- ➤ Didn't seem to care
- ➤ Was obviously in a hurry
- ➤ Was distracted by numerous things that did not seem urgent
- ➤ Was interrupted by employees asking questions
- ➤ Answered the telephone while keeping you waiting
- ➤ Appeared busy and wanting to get back to other work duties

A properly conducted interview can provide important information about an applicant, and it is a very effective screening tool. An effective interview will reveal those applicants who are not suitable for a position, enabling you to avoid wasting valuable time and money and allowing the applicant to resume looking for a suitable position. A meaningful interview is one that is not rushed, interrupted, or otherwise carried out in a distracted or unfriendly manner.

Interview Applicants Effectively

Here are some procedures which will help you conduct an effective interview. Answer the questions posed after each step.

Step 1: Help make the applicant feel comfortable. What can you do to make an applicant feel relaxed during an interview?

____

____

Step 2: Ask specific questions relating to previous employment. (For example, you may want to ask applicants about their first or most recent job, what they liked and disliked about the job, and why they left.) List two questions you might ask an applicant about previous employment.

____

____

Step 3: Ask some open-ended questions for which there are no "right" or "wrong" answers. These kinds of questions help you better understand applicants. Examples of open-ended questions include "What are your career goals?" and "How would you manage two tight deadlines if only one could be reasonably met?" List two open-ended questions that you could ask of applicants.

1. ____

____

2. ____

____

Step 4: Invite applicants to ask questions to clarify all job-related concerns.

Step 5: Tell any applicant when you will make an employment decision and always inform the applicant at least by that time.

Tip 43: Use Appropriate Applicant Tests

What comes to mind when you hear the term test? Do you think about an elaborate multi-part examination you may have had in school? Do you think about using equipment, tools, or supplies to demonstrate or perform a skill? Depending on the position for which you are seeking an experienced applicant, a test may fall into any of these categories. Following is a list of possible "tests" that might be used when hiring an applicant with presumed experience for selected positions:

Position	Sample Test
Cook	Ask about ingredients and preparation methods for a white sauce.
Cashier	Ask about procedures to authorize a credit card transaction (or ask the applicant to demonstrate).
Butcher	Ask about meat cuts taken from various sections of a beef carcass.
Auto Mechanic	Ask questions relating to diagnostic procedures.
Sales Clerk	Ask about a time when the person handled a difficult customer. What did the applicant say and/or do?
General Worker	Ask about a time when the applicant was a member of a successful team. Why was it successful? How did the applicant contribute to the team?
Clerical	Ask the applicant to compose and type a letter or to proofread a document.

Keep in mind that any test you create as a condition for employment must be administered to all applicants for that position.

Assessing Applicant Skills

What specific questions can you ask, and/or what skills can you request be demonstrated, to help assess an applicant's ability to fill an open position?

Position: ______________________________

Questions and/or physical tests: ______________________________

____

____

____

Position: ______________________________

Questions and/or physical tests: ______________________________

____

____

____

Tip 44: Check Applicant References

Years ago, checking the references of former employers could often yield a great deal of useful information about an applicant, which could significantly affect the selection process. One might learn, for example, about problems the employee had that led to discharge. Personal qualities–both good and those less desirable–were often revealed.

Today, former employers and other professional references are much less likely to provide this type of personal information because of fear of lawsuits. Attorneys specializing in labor law frequently suggest that former employers supply no information other than verification of employment dates and the position held.

If such minimal information is now provided, why check employee references? Because this small amount of information can mean a lot! For example, verifying dates of employment helps to identify any periods of time in the applicant's background that are unaccounted for. It also confirms that information contained in the application is correct, indicating that the applicant filled it out carefully.

Practicing making a reference call will make the task more interesting, less stressful, and more useful to you.

CHECKING AN APPLICANT'S REFERENCES

Hello, [Mr. or Ms.] ______________________.
(*Name of reference*)

My name is________________. I am a ____________________ at
(*Name of position*)

____________________________. ______________________
(*Name of your organization*) (*Name of applicant*)

has applied for the position of ______________________________.
(*Name of position*)

He/she indicated that he/she had been a _________________ at your
(*Name of position*)

organization. I am calling to confirm his/her employment with you.

Is_________________the correct title for the job he/she had with you?
(*Name of position*)

May I please confirm the dates of employment? ________ to ________.
(*Start date*) (*End date*)

Is there additional information you can provide about his/her work with you?

Thank you very much, ________________.
(*Name of reference*)

S T R A T E G Y **6**

Start Smart–Employee Selection and Orientation

Tip 45: Make a Timely Decision

Assume that you are an entry-level employee seeking a new position. It is Thursday, and you have decided to spend the morning looking for work. You stop to talk with three potential employers, two of whom express great interest in you as an employee. The first prospective employer makes a definite offer and states that you can begin work the following Monday; the second prospective employer informs you that he or she will *call you* the following Monday with an employment decision. Both employers offer similar pay and benefits, working conditions, and opportunities for advancement. Would you accept the job offer of the first employer to begin on Monday? Most job seekers would take the first offer that was made!

In the past, the conventional advice for managers has been to be very cautious in offering employment too readily to those who apply for work. In today's competitive market, you must be prepared to offer employment immediately.

Once you have made a tentative decision, let the applicant know that you are, in fact, hiring him or her subject to any conditions you place on hiring decisions. These conditions may include items such as successful completion of drug screening (see Tip 47), provision of required identity documents, a review of background or reference checks, approval of a bonding company, or any other factors important to you. By doing this, you can rescind the offer if needed, but you have filled the open position virtually "on-the-spot."

Determine Your Conditions of Employment

List the factors that must be successfully addressed before a formal job offer can be made in your organization. Indicate the amount of time normally needed to address these issues.

Pre-Employment Essential Conditions	**Time Needed to Address Essential Conditions**
______________________________	____________________
______________________________	____________________
______________________________	____________________
______________________________	____________________

Use the preceding information to develop a "Pre-Approval Work Offer" form. (You may want to revise the sample form that follows.)

Pre-Approval Work Offer Form

Prior to implementing this document, check with your human resource department or attorney to confirm that it adheres to any applicable employment laws in your area.

____
(*Name of your organization*)

This is to inform __________________________ that the position of
(*Name of applicant*)

________________ is being offered subject to the following conditions:
(*Job title*)

1. ____

2. ____

3. ____

The first day of employment will be ____________________; starting compensation will be _______________. It is expected that all information needed to make a final job offer will be available by _________________.
(*Date*)

The terms included in this Pre-Approval Work Offer do not, in any way, affect your "employment at will" status.

____
(*Manager's signature*)

Tip 46: Seek Attitude Before Skills

Many managers prefer to hire employees who are already well trained for the jobs for which they are hired. In reality, however, nearly all new employees must be taught how you do things in your organization. Therefore, it is important that the employees you select have a positive, enthusiastic attitude about your organization and the training you will provide. Most work skills can be learned if the learner is willing and the trainer invests the proper amount of time in planning for and delivering training.

Without the proper attitude toward learning, training will be ineffective, leading to unwanted turnover. Despite your preference for hiring pre-trained staff, remember to focus on an applicant's attitude before you evaluate current skills. You can teach new skills to a willing employee. Attitudes, on the other hand, are preformed ideas already held by the applicant. If they can be changed, this will only happen over time. The reality is that you simply may not have the time needed to change an employee's attitude before he or she leaves your organization.

Attitude Experiences

Think about your own experience as a supervisor. Recall an employee who didn't have the required knowledge or skills when he or she was hired, but had a great attitude.

Was the employee able to obtain the knowledge or skills necessary to adequately perform the job? ❑ Yes ❑ No

Did he or she turn out to be a good employee? ❑ Yes ❑ No

Would you hire that individual (or others like him/her) again? ❑ Yes ❑ No

If you answered "no" to any of the preceding questions, consider how you could have anticipated the new employee's performance, based on what you observed at the time.

____

____

____

Now recall another employee who had the required knowledge or skills but who didn't care about the job, other employees, or customers; in other words, an employee who didn't have the proper attitude.

Did he or she turn out to be a good employee? ❑ Yes ❑ No

Do you agree that it is best to hire for attitude and then teach the required knowledge or skills? ❑ Yes ❑ No

Why or why not?

____

____

____

Tip 47: Implement Drug Testing

Employees who use drugs have a negative effect on your organization. They are more than three times as likely to injure themselves or another person in a workplace accident, and over five times more likely to be injured in an accident away from the job than are their non-drug-using counterparts. Drug users are also five times more likely to file a worker's compensation claim and 2.5 times more likely to have absences of eight days or more. As claims rise, so do insurance costs.

The legal conditions allowing drug testing vary by state, so it is best to seek the advice of qualified legal counsel before you begin your program. However, voluntary drug testing is legal in all states. Properly done, you will save money, increase productivity, and increase employee retention rates.

Inform Yourself About Drug Testing

For more information about drug testing, contact The Drug and Alcohol Industry Testing Association. You can find them online at www.datia.org.

You should also check out the National Clearinghouse for Alcohol and Drug Information at www.health.org/govcubs/workit/index.htm. This site provides a useful fact sheet called *Making Your Workplace Drug Free: A Kit for Employers.* It includes a form that can be printed for applicants' signatures and for existing employees' signatures (who may also be subject to random drug testing or to a drug test for cause). A summary report of drug testing laws can be found at the U.S. Department of Labor Web site: www.notes.dol.gov/said.nsf.

Tip 48: Keep Your Recruitment Package Updated

After using your recruitment package for a while to find new employees, periodically review its design and content. Remember to include your staff in this process, just as you did when the information was first developed. Find out from newly hired staff how, if at all, this information can be updated or otherwise improved. Your recruitment efforts should be continuous and directed if you want to become or remain an employer of choice in your community. The initial development of the recruitment package was a beginning step on your journey. Keep moving!

Revising Your Recruitment Package

Review (and revise as necessary) your current recruitment package by completing the following table.

Package Element	Continue to Include		If Yes, Changes Needed		If Yes, What Changes Are Needed?	Deadline for Revisions
	Yes	No	Yes	No		

Tip 49: Put It in Writing!

Now what? You have "gotten the word out" through effective recruitment tactics about positions available in your organization. You have screened applicants and implemented methods to help you wisely select employees. You have found an applicant who you *know* will be successful. What's next? Make an offer and put it in writing. This will help to ensure that there are no "surprises" that could lead, at best, to a dissatisfied employee; and, at worst, to still another vacant position.

Would you like to know exactly what your new employees believe to be the terms of their employment agreement? You probably would; and your new employees want to know exactly what you believe them to be as well. First, tell them. Second, write it down.

Create a Job Offer Form

Following is a sample job offer form that you might find useful. You can use it as is or modify it to better reflect your needs. If applicable, you will want to seek advice from your own manager, a human resources department representative, or another official before using it.

Date: ______________

To: ____
(Name of applicant)

From: ____
(Your name or company name)

Subject: Employment Offer

We are pleased to offer you employment in the following position:

____
(Name of position)

This offer is subject to the following terms and conditions:

The beginning rate of pay is: ______________________.

This position is: ❑ Full-time ❑ Part-time
and requires approximately ________ hours weekly.

The position normally involves work at the following times:

❑ Days

❑ Evenings

❑ Overnight

❑ Weekends

❑ Holidays

MORE

MORE

Overtime is paid at the following rate ____________ and is granted in the following situations:

____

____

Information on benefits is attached. [Insert applicable information from your Employee Handbook.]

Policies and procedures applicable to this position are attached. [Insert applicable information from your Employee Handbook.]

Pre-employment conditions to be met as conditions of this offer include the following (identify drug screening results, reference verification, and/or other pre-employment conditions):

____

____

Other information applicable to this job offer includes the following:

____

____

Please respond to this job offer by: __________________________

(*Date/time*)

_________________________________ ____________________

(*Manager's name*) (*Date*)

Tip 50: Conduct a Post-Hiring Interview

The individuals who join your work team can be a valuable source of information about you, your organization, and your recruiting strategies. The time you spend collecting and maintaining this information, and then using it, will be very cost-effective.

The procedures you use to collect this information need not be complex or time-consuming for either you or the new employee. Create a simple questionnaire that asks new employees the "newspaper reporter's questions" about their employment decision.

Pre-Hiring Interview

New employee's name: ______________________________

What factors made you decide to apply to our organization? __________

____

Where did you hear that we were hiring? ______________________________

____

When did you decide to accept our offer? ______________________________

Why did you decide to accept our offer? ______________________________

____

How could we change our recruitment and selection process to make it easier for others to apply for a position with our organization?

____

____

WANTED: YOUR RECRUITMENT IDEAS

We hope you'll share your creative ideas about how to recruit and select employees. If you modify or improve upon a strategy or tip in this book, or create new tips that might be shared with fellow supervisors and managers, we would like to hear about your suggestions.

Feel free to use and copy this form, and send or fax it to us.

Tip:

____

____

____

Implementation suggestions:

____

____

____

Your name and address:

____

____

____

If we use your idea in another book, we will cite you as the contributor and send you a complimentary copy.

Please send to:

Jack Ninemeier
c/o The Eli Broad Graduate School of Management
Michigan State University
239 Epply Center
East Lansing, Michigan, 48824-1124
Fax: 517-432-1170
Email: ninemeie@msu.edu

Additional Reading

Ahlrichs, Nancy. *Competing for Talent: Key Recruitment and Retention Strategies for Becoming an Employer of Choice.* Palo Alto, CA: Davies-Black Pub., 2000.

Arthur, Diane. *Recruiting, Interviewing, Selecting & Orienting New Employees.* NY: AMACOM, 1998.

Cook, Mary F., editor. *The AMA Handbook for Employee Recruitment and Retention.* NY: American Management Association, 1992.

Fitzwater, Terry L. *Behavior-Based Interviewing.* Menlo Park, CA: Crisp Publications, 2000.

Maddux, Robert. *Quality Interviewing.* Menlo Park, CA: Crisp Publications, 1994.

Smart, Bradford. *Topgrading: How Leading Companies Win by Hiring, Coaching, and Keeping the Best People.* Paramus, NJ: Prentice Hall Press, 1999.

Still, Del. *High Impact Hiring: How to Interview and Select Outstanding Employees.* Dana Point, CA: Management Development Systems, 1997.

Wendover, Robert. *High Performance Hiring.* Menlo Park, CA: Crisp Publications, 1991.

Wood, Robert. *Competency-Based Recruitment and Selection.* Chichester, NY: Wiley, 1998.

CRISP WORLDWIDE DISTRIBUTION

English language books are distributed worldwide. Major international distributors include:

ASIA/PACIFIC

Australia/New Zealand: In Learning, PO Box 1051, Springwood QLD, Brisbane, Australia 4127 Tel: 61-7-3-841-2286, Facsimile: 61-7-3-841-2618 ATTN: Messrs. Gordon

Philippines: National Book Store, Inc., Quad Alpha Centrum Bldg, 125 Pioneer Street, Mandaluyong, Metro Manila, Philippines Tel: 632-631-8051, Facsimile: 632-631-5016

Singapore, Malaysia, Brunei, Indonesia: Times Book Shops. Direct sales HQ: STP Distributors, Pasir Panjang Distrientre, Block 1 #03-01A, Pasir Panjang Rd. Singapore 118480 Tel: 65-2767626, Facsimile: 65-2767119

Japan: Phoenix Associates Co., Ltd., Mizuho Bldng, 3-F, 2-12-2, Kami Osaki, Shinagawa-Ku, Tokyo 141 Tel: 81-33-443-7231, Facsimile: 81-33-443-7640 ATTN: Mr. Peter Owans

CANADA

Crisp Learning Canada, 60 Briarwood Avenue, Mississauga, ON L5G 3N6 Canada Tel: 905-274-5678, Facsimile: 905-278-2801 ATTN: Mr. Steve Connolly

Trade Book Stores: Raincoast Books, 8680 Cambie Street, Vancouver, BC V6P 6M9 Canada Tel: 604-323-7100, Facsimile: 604-323-2600 ATTN: Order Desk

EUROPEAN UNION

England: Flex Training, Ltd., 9-15 Hitchin Street, Baldock, Hertfordshire, SG7 6A, England Tel: 44-1-46-289-6000, Facsimile: 44-1-46-289-2417 ATTN: Mr. David Willetts

INDIA

Multi-Media HRD, Pvt., Ltd., National House, Tulloch Road, Appolo Bunder, Bombay, India 400-039 Tel: 91-22-204-2281, Facsimile: 91-22-283-6478 ATTN: Messrs. Aggarwal

SOUTH AMERICA

Mexico: Grupo Editorial Iberoamerica, Nebraska 199, Col. Napoles, 03810 Mexico, D.F. Tel: 525-523-0994, Facsimile: 525-543-1173 ATTN: Señor Nicholas Grepe

SOUTH AFRICA

Alternative Books, PO Box 1345, Ferndale 2160, South Africa Tel: 27-11-792-7730, Facsimile: 27-11-792-7787 ATTN: Mr. Vernon de Haas